FRIEDRICH HÖLDERLIN
# SELECTED POEMS

# FRIEDRICH HÖLDERLIN

# Selected Poems

translated by
DAVID CONSTANTINE

BLOODAXE BOOKS

ISBN: 1 85224 064 4

First published 1990 by
Bloodaxe Books Ltd,
P.O. Box 1SN,
Newcastle upon Tyne NE99 1SN


Bloodaxe Books Ltd acknowledges
the financial assistance of Northern Arts.

ACKNOWLEDGEMENTS

Cover portrait of Hölderlin (1786) reproduced
by kind permission of Württembergische Landesbibliothek
Stuttgart: Hölderlin-Archiv (Cod. poet. fol. 63 V b 3).

Extracts from the Sophocles translations
first appeared in *PN Review*.


Typesetting by EMS Phototypesetting, Berwick upon Tweed.

Printed in Great Britain by
Billings & Sons Limited, Worcester.

# Contents

7    *Introduction*

13    'When I was a boy'
14    To Diotima
15    Diotima
16    Plea for Forgiveness
17    'Another day'
18    To the Sun God
19    To the Fates
20    Fate. Hyperion's Song
21    Sung under the Alps
22    The Archipelago
30    Homecoming
33    The Rhine
39    Patmos
45    Remembrance
47    The Ister
49    Mnemosyne
51    Tears
52    Ganymede
53    Chiron
55    Ages of Life
56    Half of Life
57    'As birds slowly pass over'
58    'As upon seacoasts'
59    Home
60    'For when the juice of the vine'
61    'On pale leaves'
62    'When over the vineyard'
63    The Eagle
64    'Where we began'
65    'Severed and at a distance now'
67    FROM Sophocles' *Ajax*
70    FROM Sophocles' *Antigone*
73    'In a lovely blue'

75    *Notes*

# Introduction

Hölderlin was born in 1770, as were also Wordsworth, Hegel and Beethoven. That generation grew up believing the world – 'the very world, which is the world/ Of all of us' – could be changed for the better, and that love, reason and justice could be instituted in it, here and now. They were disappointed. But disappointment does not annul hope. What we can still get from Hölderlin, as from Wordsworth, is a passionate and generous hope. That survives, in the teeth of every disappointment. Hölderlin, writing his best poems after things had gone badly wrong in France and after the possibility of improvement in Germany had been erased, constantly offers images and visions of fulfilled humanity. True, the poems demonstrate the *absence* of fulfilment; but their project is utopian and it is their drive towards fulfilment which lingers in the blood after reading them. That feeling is an equivalent of what it was like to be alive then, when 'the whole earth/ The beauty wore of promise'. The excitement and the faith revive.

Hölderlin was born into the so-called *Ehrbarkeit*, the Respectability, who administered Church and State. He was brought up by an anxious mother, his father, then his stepfather, having died before he was nine. He was brought up in and never quite escaped from a condition of dependence. First on his mother: though in fact comfortably off and with a large inheritance to pass on to her eldest son, she kept him throughout his life in want of funds and he never broke free. Secondly on the State: he was put through a church education free, on condition that he serve the State (through its Church) once educated. He spent his life resisting that obligation. He was schooled in theology, but also in philosophy and the classics. He took all three very seriously, and the tensions that engendered were hard to manage. He entered the seminary in Tübingen in 1788 and suffered there, with his eyes on France, as though it was the oppressive and anachronistic State in miniature. He had Schelling and Hegel with him as allies in republicanism.

Hölderlin was born in Lauffen, north of Stuttgart, but grew up in Nürtingen, also on the Neckar but south of the city. All his education was in Swabia – in Denkendorf, Maulbronn and Tübingen – and it was to Tübingen, to the clinic, that he was forcibly returned, and all the latter half of his life he spent in a tower in the town walls with a view of the river and the meadows and hills beyond. Swabia was his homeland. He sought employment outside it (he had to, or the Church would have claimed him) but when those employments failed he returned. He idealised the homeland as the paradise of childhood and as the location for the New Republic; but in fact, until his collapse, he was debarred from settling in it. That fact, like so much in Hölderlin's life, is intrinsically figurative.

Hölderlin imagined his ideal largely in Greek terms. Quite simply, the civilisation of Periclean Athens seemed to him the best the human race had ever achieved and he wanted an equivalent of it for his own day and age and even believed the French Revolution might bring it about. Once disappointed, he risked becoming merely nostalgic, for an ideal sited irretrievably in the past. He countered that by committing himself to the present, to present time and to present place, and by imagining an ideal future for them. He created poem by poem a world having two poles: Greece, and what he called Hesperia. And the heart of Hesperia was his own homeland Swabia. He celebrates the world north of the Alps, his own world, its towns and hills and above all its rivers, as a land fit for the ideal, once realised in Greece, to be welcomed into; and again and again he connects Greece, now lost, with Hesperia, still to come. That way of thinking – an ideal past, an unsatisfactory present, an ideal future – was characteristic of Hölderlin's age; but the expression he gave to it was peculiarly concrete and precise. He embodied his poetic thinking in landscapes: in those he knew well (having walked through them), and in others, the Greek, which he had only read about in publications by French and English travellers. A similar luminousness lies over both zones.

When Hölderlin finished his education in 1793 he took immediate steps to avoid being drafted into the Church. He went "abroad", that is, outside Swabia, and became a house-tutor. In all he had four such jobs. It was the usual thing for a young man to do if he wished really to be furthering his own intellectual and artistic life; but it was a compromise and not a happy one. His task was to educate the children of the well-to-do. In that paid capacity he was a domestic, and liable always to be treated accordingly. But by his talents and his sensibility he was the superior of his employers. The predicament of the house-tutor was in epitome the predicament of artists and intellectuals altogether in Germany at that time: marginalised and dependent. They added culture to a household, as ornament and extra. In that they were allied naturally with the women, whose role also was subordinate and ornamental. Hölderlin's second post was in Frankfurt, the bankers' city. There he saw the spirit denigrated and pushed to the periphery. He saw money triumphant.

Hölderlin's employer in Frankfurt was a man called Jakob Gontard whose motto, despite being married to a beautiful, cultivated and intelligent woman, was 'Business first'. When Hölderlin came into that household he and Susette, as natural allies, the woman and the poet, fell in love. She became the Diotima of his poems and proof to him that ideal life was possible on earth. Loving and being loved by her he was, for a time, in a condition of fulfilled humanity. The ideal was realised, then lost. They were severed, she died, his mind collapsed. Her existence in Frankfurt, in the very city of mercantile dreadful night, seemed miraculous. She was Greece recovered and restored to life, she was the woman fit for the New Age. When in France the attempt to change the institutions failed, bringing a new tyranny, many idealists put their hopes in a change of hearts and minds instead. Susette in herself seemed to Hölderlin a guarantor of what humanity had been like and might be like again.

Hölderlin found his own poetic voice when he met Susette. Prior to that he had been much under the influence of other writers, notably Schiller (whom he adulated). He was writing a novel, *Hyperion*, when he came to Frankfurt; he re-wrote it when he met her. Its heroine is called Diotima. Forgive me, he said, giving her the second volume, that Diotima dies. The book was dedicated to Susette Gontard. Forced out of her house in September 1798 Hölderlin moved to nearby Homburg and there, for a while, lived on his earnings and tried to make his own way. He reflected on his art and began to write the poems for which he is best known. And he worked at a tragedy, *Empedocles*, pushing it through three versions, to no completion. Away from Susette, in Nürtingen, Switzerland and Bordeaux, he wrote the elegies, 'Bread and Wine', 'Homecoming', and the great hymns in Pindar's style, 'The Rhine', 'Germania' and, later, 'Patmos'. A whole unique *oeuvre* was produced. There cannot have been many days during his brief maturity when he was not writing at poems among the very best in German literature. It is a tremendous work, like nobody else's, his in every line and in its large project.

In the winter of 1801-02 Hölderlin walked to Bordeaux, over the Auvergne. He took up a job as house-tutor there, his last; but left in May and went home, via Paris (where he saw the classical statues Napoleon had stolen from Italy). Susette died in June, of German measles caught whilst nursing her children. When Hölderlin showed himself in Stuttgart and Nürtingen his friends and family thought him out of his mind. But it is not known for certain whether or not he had already learned Susette was dead. Thereafter, for four years until his incarceration in the clinic, he struggled against fatigue and distraction, and wrote marvellous poems – 'Patmos', for example, 'Mnemosyne' and 'Remembrance'. He held a sinecure in Homburg, as librarian to the *Landgraf*, and it was from there that he was transported in September 1806, having become, so it was said, too difficult to manage in that little town. He had eight months in the clinic, and was discharged then as incurable with 'at most three years' to live. He lived another thirty-six, half his life, in good hands, in the loving and sensible care of a carpenter's family. He became a celebrity, sightseers visited him and asked him for verses, which he readily gave. They are rhyming verses, and he signed them with strange names. Yes, he was much visited, by the ghoulish and by the truly devoted. He died peacefully in 1843.

Hölderlin is the poet of absence. His gods have departed, presence has been lost. There is no poet more honest and uncompromising in the depiction of absence and loss. Reading Hölderlin we *know* what bereavement, in its widest sense, is like. But we know also, with an equal or greater force, what fulfilment would be like, what it would be like to live lives full of love and joy; and the injunction of his poetry, always there, is to believe in the possibility of that fulfilment and to seek to make it real.

I have tried, in making this selection, to give new readers of Hölderlin some idea of the nature of his poems; but those who already know him will miss many favourites. In Michael Hamburger's *Poems and Fragments* (Cambridge University Press, 1980) will be found almost the whole corpus of Hölderlin's poetry, in German and English, and I am glad to be able to direct readers to that excellent volume. Here I have ordered the poems more or less chronologically but with an eye also to giving variety if they are read through consecutively.

Hamburger thinks of himself as a "mimetic" translator; that is, he has reproduced very exactly not only the sense but also the forms – the verses, the lines, the metrics – of the originals. I have kept close, but not so close. In translating the odes ('To the Fates', for example, or 'Plea for Forgiveness') I adopted their syllabic count but not their metres; for the elegy 'Homecoming' and for the long poem 'The Archipelago' I attempted quite near but not exact equivalents of hexameters and pentameters; and for the hymns I imitated Hölderlin's rhythms, which are free, and allowed myself only as many lines as he used. Beyond that, I went for equivalence of effect rather than exact reproduction of the means of the effects. I knew the undertaking would be a difficult one. I learned just *how* difficult as I worked. It is hard for me to judge whether a reader having no German and coming to Hölderlin through my translations will get *any* sense of the beauty, power and poignancy of his poems. I can only hope so.

DAVID CONSTANTINE

## 'When I was a boy'

When I was a boy
  A god often rescued me
    From the shouts and the rods of men
      And I played among trees and flowers
        Secure in their kindness
          And the breezes of heaven
            Were playing there too.

And as you delight
The hearts of plants
When they stretch towards you
With little strength

So you delighted the heart in me
Father Helios, and like Endymion
I was your favourite,
Moon. O all

You friendly
And faithful gods
I wish you could know
How my soul has loved you.

Even though when I called to you then
It was not yet with names, and you
Never named me as people do
As though they knew one another

I knew you better
Than I have ever known them.
I understood the stillness above the sky
But never the words of men.

Trees were my teachers
Melodious trees
And I learned to love
Among flowers.

I grew up in the arms of the gods.

# To Diotima

Come and look at the happiness: trees in the cooling breezes
      Are tossing their branches
Like dancers' hair and with sunshine and rain the sky
      Is playing on the earth
As though joy had hands and were raising a loud music
      And light and shadows
Pass in succession and harmony over the hills
      Away like the myriad
Notes that swarm in a loving quarrel
      Over a lute.
Gently the sky has touched his brother the river
      With silvery drops
And now he is near and he empties wholly the fullness
      Held in his heart
Over the trees and the river and...

And verdant copses, the sky's own face on the river
      Fades and we lose them,
The head of the mountain, alone, the little houses, the rocks
      He hides in his lap
And the hills that assemble around him like lambs
      Clothed in blossom
As soft as wool and that suck on the clear cold
      Springs of the mountain,
The misting floor with its seed and flowers,
      The garden here,
Close things and distant leave us and wane in a happy confusion,
      The sun goes out.
But now with a rush the floods of heaven have passed
      And purer, younger,
The earth with her lucky children steps from the bath.
      In livelier joy
The green of the leaves shines forth and the brighter gold of the
                         flowers...

White as the sheep that the shepherd has flung in the dip...

# Diotima

You are silent, you suffer it. They cannot grasp
  A life lived nobly. You cast down your eyes,
    Silent in lovely daylight. You will look
      In vain for your kindred under the sun,

Those royal people who, like brothers and like
  The sociable tops of trees in a grove,
    Enjoyed home and their loves once and their
      Forever-embracing heaven and who

Sang in their hearts and never forgot their source –
  I mean the grateful, the only loyal ones,
    The bringers of joy into the depths
      Of Tartarus, men like gods, the free men,

Gentle and strong, who are souls below now
  Whom the heart has wept for since the mourning year
    Began and the stars that were there then
      Daily turn us to thinking of them still

And this lament for the dead can never rest.
  Time heals, though. Now the gods in heaven are strong
    And quick. And Nature is assuming
      Surely her old and joyful rights again.

See, love, it will happen before our hill is
  Levelled and before my words are dead the day
    Will have come when you will be named with
      Gods and heroes, a day that is like you.

## Plea for Forgiveness

Often I've lost you the golden tranquillity
  Of Heaven, yours by nature, and what you have had
    From me are many of life's
      More secret and deeper sorrows.

Forget them now and forgive me and like the cloud
  Over the peaceful moon there I shall pass and you
    Will be what you were and shine
      In your beauty, beloved light.

## 'Another day'

Another day. I follow another path,
   Enter the leafing woodland, visit the spring
      Or the rocks where the roses bloom
         Or search from a look-out, but nowhere

Love are you to be seen in the light of day
   And down the wind go the words of our once so
      Beneficent conversation...

Your beloved face has gone beyond my sight,
   The music of your life is dying away
      Beyond my hearing and all the songs
         That worked a miracle of peace once on

My heart, where are they now? It was long ago,
   So long and the youth I was has aged nor is
      Even the earth that smiled at me then
         The same. Farewell. Live with that word always.

For the soul goes from me to return to you
   Day after day and my eyes shed tears that they
      Cannot look over to where you are
         And see you clearly ever again.

## To the Sun God

Where are you? The soul is shadowy in me
   And drunk on your happiness. A moment since
      I saw a dazzling god, like a young
         Man tired at the finish of a journey,

Bathing the hair of his head in golden clouds
   And my eyes cannot keep from looking where he went.
      He has left us now, he has gone to
         Lands where they love him still and revere him.

I love you, earth, for you are grieving with me
   And our grief like the troubles of children turns
      Into sleep and just as the breezes
         Flutter and whisper in the strings until

More adept fingers coax a better music
   Out of them so mists and dreams play over us
      Until the loved one comes and life and
         The spirit are kindled in us again.

## To the Fates

Give me one summer, you with the power to,
  Only one, and an autumn of song, so that
    My heart having fed to its content
      On music will be happier dying.

A soul withheld its heavenly right in life
  Will be restless in Orcus too; but let
    The making of the holiest thing
      My heart wants, the poem, be given me

Welcome then the silence of the world of shades!
  I am at peace, although my music may not
    Accompany me down. Once I'll have
      Lived like the gods and more I'm not asking.

## Fate. Hyperion's Song


You inhabit the light, you walk
  On easy ground, the shining
    Breezes of Heaven play
      Around you, the blessed,
        As lightly as the lyre-
          Playing fingers of a girl.

Gods have no fate, they have
  The sleeping infant's
    Quiet breath;
      Their spirits, kept
        From spoiling in the bud,
        Blossom for ever;
          They have a still
          Eternal clarity
          Of gaze.

We have no footing anywhere,
  No rest, we topple,
    Fall and suffer
      Blindly from hour
      To hour like water
      Pitched from fall
      To fall, year in,
        Year out, headlong,
        Ignorant.

# Sung under the Alps

Holy innocence, the best beloved, the
Closest to the heart of gods and men, indoors
Or under the sky where you sit at the feet
                             Of them, the elders,

Wise and wanting nothing; for although we know
All manner of good we stare like beasts still
Often at Heaven, but how pure to you, pure
                             Yourself, are all things.

Look at the brute beast of the fields: it serves
You willingly and trusts you, the dumb woods speak,
As they did formerly, their words to you and
                             The mountains teach you

Holy laws, and whatever to us who are
Experienced the almighty now, the Father,
Lets be made clear, only you may utter it
                             Shining innocence.

To be thus alone with the gods, light passing
By and the rivers and the wind and time that
Hurries to its end, and yet to be steady-
                             Eyed before them

Is blessed, I know nothing more, nor want, so long
As the flood that uproots the willow does not
Take me too and I must go with the waters
                             Cradled and sleeping.

Who truly houses God in his heart of hearts
Is content at home; in freedom then, so long
As I may let me sing and elucidate
                             The tongues of Heaven.

# The Archipelago

Are the cranes coming home to you? Are the ships
Resuming their course to your shores? Do breaths of the breezes
We longed for move on your quietened waves? Does the dolphin,
Lured from the depths, sun his back in the daylight again?
Is Ionia in flower? Is it time? In spring
When the living take heart and their first love
Revives and the memory of golden times then always
You draw me. I come. I salute you: age-old and silent.

You live as you were, unlessened, the mountains lend you
Shade to lie in, you embrace with the arms of a youth still
A beautiful land, and of all your daughters, father,
Of all the flowering islands, not one has been lost.
Crete stands and grassy Salamis and Delos lifts from among
Dark laurels spiked with light at every dawn
Her ecstatic head and Tenos has and Chios
Purple fruits in abundance, on drunken hills
The Cyprian drink wells up and from off Calauria silver
Streams fall, as they always did, into the sea, their father.
All live still, all the mothers of heroes, the islands,
Flowering from year to year, and though the abyss let loose
Sometimes a flame in the dark, a nether tempest, and seized
One hold and she died and sank in your cherishing lap,
You lasted, for much has gone down and
Risen in your depths and your darkness, sea-god.

Also the gods who inhabit the heights and the stillness
Far off, and who bring with the largesse of power
Sleep and the cheerful daylight and dreaming thoughts
Over the heads of sentient men, they are what they were:
Your companions, and often when evening falls
And over the mountains of Asia the holy moonlight
Lifts and the stars encounter themselves in your waves
You shine as if it were Heaven lighting you
Under the travelling stars and your waters switch and your brothers'
Lullaby above echoes from your loving heart.
Then when the light comes, star of the east, the wonderworker,
When the daystar comes and illuminates all things
And the living begin their lives in the golden dream

That the sun, like a poet, presents them with daily
For you in your grief his magic is kinder still,
Kinder than his light, even more beautiful
Is the wreath that he still, as he always did, for a token,
Remembering you, winds in your wintry hair.
Heaven, clear blue, bends over you still and returns
Out of the heights your couriers, the clouds, with the gods' gift,
Lightning, and over the land you despatch them, the woods
On shore, where it burns, reel in the rain and with you
Billow and roar and soon, like a son gone astray
When his father calls, the Maeander, streaming in thousands,
Tears from its twists and turns and Cayster runs to you
Over the flats with laughter and the elder, the firstborn,
Too long hidden, your Nile, in majesty now
Strides from the mountainous distance, tall, like a triumph
Clanging with weapons, homesick and reaching for you.

    Still you think yourself lonely. Rocks in the dumb night
Hear you grieving and often the winged waves fly,
Angered, away from humans at Heaven.
You miss them, the loved ones, the noble company
Who honoured you once and wreathed your seaboards
With cities and beautiful temples. The holy elements
Always must seek and pine for, like heroes for laurels,
Hearts to be crowned in, the hearts of a feeling humanity.

    Where is Athens now? Oh, grieving god, has your city,
The one you loved best, that reached from your sacred shores,
Collapsed under ash entirely and buried even her graves?
Or are there remains, might a sailor,
Passing, remember her name and call her to mind?
Were there not columns once, risen up, and did not
The figured gods shine down from the citadel roof?
And the turbulent voice of the people murmured
Louder out of the Agora, the streets hurried down
Through the boisterous gates to your port full of blessings.
Look where the trader, thinking into the distance,
Loosed his ship with a will, the flighted breezes
Blew for him too and the gods loved him like the poets
For balancing the earth's good gifts and joining near and far.
Distant Cyprus drew him and Tyre and he reached
As high as Colchis and down the sea to old Egypt

Winning crimson and fleeces and corn and wine
For home, for his city, and often by the wings of his ship,
By his hopes, he was carried through the pillars of reckless
Hercules, out to new blessed isles – but meanwhile
Differently moved, a youth sat alone on the shore of the town,
Listened to the waves, alone in a grave enquiry,
Listened and sat at the feet of Poseidon,
The master, the breaker, and learned from the god what was needed.

For Persia, hating the spirit and lord over millions,
Year after year has stockpiled weapons and slaves,
Laughing at the land of Greece and the little islands,
Thinking them child's play. He understands slaves but not
People with lives, whose spirit the gods have armoured.
Gives the word carelessly: like fluid from Etna
Tipped when it seethes and spreading in fearful streams
And burning in crimson the cities and the flower gardens
And entering the shock of the sacred sea as a river of fire –
So with the King in a glorious riot the hordes run down,
Scorching and murderous to cities, from Ecbatana.
Athens, the beautiful, falls. Old men
Look back among listening beasts from the hills
In flight to the homes and beg for the burning temples,
Nor can the sons arouse the holy ashes with prayer
Ever again. Death on the plain. Towards Heaven
Fireclouds vanish. To reap more of the country
Hot in the face the laden Persians pass.

Off Salamis then, oh that day off Salamis!
Waiting for the end the women of Athens, the girls,
Stand, and the mothers with children, saved, in their arms,
Listening: the voice of the god in the sea, deep down,
Rises with hope and promise, the gods in the sky
Look down, weighing the verdict. For there, off the shaken land
Since dawn, like a slowly manoeuvring storm,
The battle has swung, on frothy seas, and noon strikes
Into the anger unnoticed, exactly above the fighters.
And now the men of the city, children of children of heroes,
Face more brightly, they are the gods' favourites, the issue
Is theirs, they think, and the children of Athens won't haul
Their spirit, that spits at death, in yet.
For sand may be quenching the prey's lost blood but

Still, a last time, it rises, flushed with a nobler strength,
And sets back the hunter – like that, in the row of arms,
Ordered by masters, gathered in a fury, the wild
Enemy even as they fall recover some soul.
Fighting flares up again, like wrestling men
The ships seize hold, the rudder swings with the swell,
Planking breaks as they struggle and sailors and ships sink.

  Sung silly by the day, dreaming a vanishing dream,
The King rolls his eyes, grinning all askew at the outcome,
Threatens, begs and rejoices, sends men out like lightning.
He sends them in vain. No one comes back, but
Thunderous, vengeful waves pitch without number
Bloody messengers, ships that have burst and the army's corpses
At his feet where he sits enthroned, by the shaken shore, the pauper,
Eyes on the rout, and the rabble in flight drag him with them,
He bolts, the god drives him, over the waters the god
Drives his lost squadrons and jeers and has smashed his show
To bits and found out the weakling under the armour.

  Lovingly back to the waiting abandoned river
Come the people of Athens and down from the homeland's mountains
The shining crowds, meeting like waters, replenish
The emptied plain with joy. But like a mother grown old
After years when the child she thought lost comes
Home to her bosom alive, a young man, but meanwhile
Her soul has faded in grief and the joy comes too late,
Hoping has travailed her, what he recounts,
Her loving and thankful son, she can hardly seize –
Home appears thus to the people of Athens returning.
They look for the dear gods' groves, they look without finding.
Coming as victors, where is the gate to receive them
That welcomed the wanderer with open arms when he came
Home from the islands and looked up with longing and saw
Mother Athene's citadel shining ahead?
But they know their streets when they see them: desolate,
Gardens in mourning. In the Agora then –
The Stoa's columns are prone and the gods'
Statues face down – they take hands and obeying their hearts,
Trusting to love, renew their citizenship.
And a man goes looking for house and home and finds them
Under the rubble; his wife, thinking of the heart of the house

Where they slept, weeps in his arms; the children
Ask is the table there where they sat in the family
Order, watched by the elders, the smiling gods of the household.
Now, though, the people make themselves tents; neighbourhoods
Form as they were and after the heart's own custom the airy
Houses consort on the slopes of the round of hills.
So in the meanwhile they live, like the ancients, the freemen who,
Sure of their strength and trusting the coming day,
Like migrant birds travelled from peak to peak
Singing, the forest's lords, the lords of the trekking river.
Mother Earth enfolds, as she always did, steady in her love,
Her people again and under the holy sky
They have quiet nights and mildly the breezes of childhood
Waft over the sleepers, the murmur of Ilissus
Comes through the planes to them and at night the
          waves of the sea-god,
Promising new days, whispering of new deeds, comes
Out of the distance with cheerful dreams for his favourites.
Flowers have sprung up again, little by little, and bloom
Golden on the trampled fields and believing hands
Have greened the olive again, and the horses of Athens
Pasture as before in peace on Colonus meadows.

   Honouring Mother Earth and the god of the waves
Now the city flowers, becoming a wonder, starlike,
Founded firmly, the work of the spirit that puts on gladly
Fetters of love and in shapes of its own large making
Remains itself and is the perpetual mover.
And the trees serve the man as he works, Pentelicus
And every neighbourly mountain offers him marble and ore.
Living, as he is, the work leaves his hands
Like spring, full of joy, and splendid and light as sunshine.
Drinking-fountains arise and over the hills in pure
Channels springwater hurries to the shining basin;
Dwellings shine in a row all around like banqueting heroes
Passing the common cup and the high Prytaneum
Rises, gymnasia open to the air and the gods'
Temples come into being, like a bold and holy
Thought from the blessed grove into the ether the Olympeion
Climbs towards the deathless gods, and other heavenly halls,
Mother Athena, yours too, your glorious hill out of grief
Grew with a greater pride and flowered for years and,

God of the waves, your favourites sang in a happy
Gathering frequent thanks to you on the headland again.

   Where are the children of happiness now, the believers?
Home with the distant fathers, their great days forgotten,
Strolling by Lethe, and longing won't bring them
Back into sight, you will never appear
On any of the thousand paths of the flowering earth
Like gods, wherever the search goes, and I, whom your language
Reached and the legend of you, must I grieve and grieve
And my soul go down to your shades before its time?
Let me nearer at least, where your groves are still growing
And the gods' own mountain hides its sorrow in cloud,
Let me come to Parnassus, let my wanderings end
With a sight of Castalia sparkling through the darkness of oaks
And there from a scented and blossoming bowl I will pour
Water, with my tears, on the growth of new green and to you,
Asleep, shall be given the dues of the dead.
There in the silenced vale, in Tempe, under the cliffs
I will live with you and call up your glorious names
Here to me in the night and when you appear in anger,
Ploughs having raped your graves, with the voice of the heart,
Singing its love, I will soothe your shadowy lives
And my soul will accustom itself to living with you.
Like a priest I will question the holy dead but
Question the living too, the high powers of Heaven
That pass with their years and years above our ruins,
Secure in their course, for often under the stars
Like freezing winds distraction assaults my heart
And where shall I look for counsel? The comforting
Voice in Dodona's oak was stopped long ago,
At Delphi the god is dumb and the paths are empty
And wild where once, being led by his hopes,
A questioning man climbed up to the prescient town.
But above us the light, the light still speaks to mankind,
Full of beautiful pointers, the thundering god
Cries do we think of him and the grieving waves of Poseidon
Echo it back: do we think of him ever as we did?
For gods are glad to repose on a feeling heart;
The inspiring powers, gladly as they always did,
Go with our aspirations and over the mountains of home
Rests and rules and lives the unending sky

And a people might be as they were, gathered in the Father's arms,
Loving, humanly joyful and sharing one spirit.
But alas this race of ours inhabits the night, it lives
In an Orcus, godless, every man nailed
Alone to his own affairs, in the din of work
Hearing only himself, in a crazy labour
With violent hands, unresting, pitiable, and all
Their trying, like that of the Furies, brings nothing forth.
Thus till the dream of anxiety ends and our souls
Lift up, youthful and gay, and the blessing breath of love,
As often it did when the children of Hellas flowered,
Blows through the new times and over our lightened brows
Nature's spirit again, the wanderer, the god,
Appears in golden clouds, serenely biding.
But daylight is holding off. Those born with the gods still
Inhabit, so it seems, the depths of the earth,
Lonely below, asleep, whilst an undying spring,
Unseen, is brightening over their heads.
Surely no longer! I hear in the distance that festival
Day's chorale on the green hill, the echoing groves,
Youth breathing again and the soul of the people
Collected and still in a freer song and the god
Honoured who belongs in the heights but the valleys are his too.
For where the river in its growing youth hurries out
Happily into the flowering land and the tall
Corn ripens on the sunny plain and fruit, there too
The people are wreathed with love, on the city's hill
The heavenly hall of gladness shines like a human home.
Life, all of life, has filled with the sense of God
And everywhere nature returns to her children, the old
Fulfilment returns and as if from a hill of springs
Blessings water the seedling soul of the people.
O festive Athens, o Sparta remembered for bravery,
Sweet springtime of Greece, when our
Autumn comes, when the spirits of the old world return
Ripened and the year moves to fulfilment
Then on a day that will hold the past in its arms
Weeping in thanks let the people look towards Hellas
And soften the pride of their triumph with memories.

Blossom meanwhile until our fruition begins,
Ionian gardens, blossom, and over the rubble of Athens

May greenery hide that grief from the light of day,
Laurel woods wreath with their lasting leaves the hills
Housing your dead, at Marathon, there where the boys
Won and died and there on the fields of Chaeronea
Where the last men of Athens ran with their weapons and bled
Fleeing from a shameful day, and the travelled streams
Sing down from the hills into the battle valley
Sing down from the peaks of Oeta the facts of fate.
But you, undying, though the Greeks have ceased
Singing your praise, o Poseidon, from out of your waves
Sound in my soul still, often, and on the water
My spirit will move like a swimmer, bravely, and practise
New happiness such as the gods have, and know what the gods mean
And how things change and grow, and when these tearing times
Assail my head too roughly and the need among mortal men
And bewilderment shake my mortal life
Let me think of the stillness then that you have in your depths.

# Homecoming
*for my family*

### 1

In the Alps it is still bright light and in there cloud,
　Dreaming up joyful things, covers the valley mouth.
Hither and thither is flung and falls the jesting air of the mountain,
　Down through firs the abrupt light flashes and fades.
Slow haste, cold shivers of joy: Chaos is working,
　Young in shape but strong, revels in loving strife
Under the scarp, it ferments, it reels in the eternal confines,
　Morning is coming up, God's dancers are rising.
For the funds of the year are deepest in there and the holy
　Hours, the days, ordered and mixed more boldly.
But the storm bird watches time, between mountains
　High in the air he holds steady and calls out the day.
Now too, deep in the depths, the village has woken and looks
　Fearlessly, trusting the heights, up from under the peaks,
Scenting growth, for already, like lightnings, the ancient water
　Sources are tumbling, the ground, under their beating, steams.
Echo resounds: by day and by night a measureless
　Work of donation comes forth from the hands of that place.

### 2

Light meanwhile rests on the silvery heights over all,
　Up there the shining snow is already strewn with roses.
Higher still, over the light, the god, in his clarity,
　Lives and his lucid joy lifts on the play of its rays.
His life is alone and still, his face shines brightly, he seems
　Leaning to lend us life out of his heights of sky,
Creative of joy, with us, as often when, knowing the measure,
　Sparing us, holding off, knowing our limit of breath,
He sends the cities and houses a wellshaped fortune,
　Mild rains to open the land, teeming clouds and these
Familiar breezes and such sweet springtimes as this,
　Slowly his hands lifting up mourners towards joy again,
When he, the maker, renews the times and re-enters
　Freshly hearts in the stillness of ageing and works
Down and down and opens and brightens, which is
　What he loves and a life starts again here and now,
Grace, as it once did, blossoms and into our present comes
　Spirit, and courage and joy rise on wings again.

### 3

I said many things to him, for whatever poets
    Think and sing is mostly the angels' and his;
And I asked many things for my country to keep the
    Spirit from befalling us suddenly and unasked;
Also for you, many things, who in my country are anxious,
    Who welcome the exiles home smiling with their debt of thanks,
People of my land, for you. I was lulled by the lake, the boatman
    Sat in the stern at his ease, lauding our progress.
Over the levels of the lake one joyous movement extended
    Under the sails and now there in the daybreak the town
Blossoms and brightens forth and from under the shadowy Alps,
    Bringing them in, the boat enters and rests in the port.
The shores here are warm and the open and welcoming valleys,
    Beautifully lit by paths, face me in shimmering green.
Gardens are grouped together, bright buds are starting,
    Birdsong excites in a man love of the open road.
Everything looks wellknown, the hurried greeting in passing
    Seems a friend's and the faces all seem familiar.

### 4

This is the ground I was born in, the ground of my home,
    What you are looking for hurries to meet you here.
And a travelled man stands like a son in a din
    Of waves at the gate, staring and seeking names
Fair enough for you, in songs, and calling you blessed
    Lindau, one of the land's welcoming doors that lead us
Out where the distances promise so much, where the
    Wonders are, where God's wild animal, the Rhine,
Breakneck out of the heights comes down to the levels
    And the valley with a shout shows from among the rocks –
To enter there and to stride the bright mountains towards Como
    Or follow the daylight down the length of the open lake.
But I am led in at that door on a sacred way
    Home on familiar roads under blossoming trees
To visit the land and the lovely vales of the Neckar,
    The woods, the green sanctum, oaks and the tranquil
Birches and beeches together in a company where
    Among hills a place lovingly captures me.

## 5

There I'm received. My mother, the town, when they speak
    Touch and awaken things the heart learned long ago.
Still the same things! Oh my loved ones, the sunlight and joy
    Flower for you still and your eyes almost never were brighter.
All as it was, thriving and ripening, but nothing
    That lives there and loves loses its loyalty.
Meanwhile the best, to be found, is lying under
    God's bow of peace, put by for young and old.
I speak like a fool. Joy makes me. Tomorrow and when we
    Visit the living fields, outside, in future,
Under the trees in blossom in the holidays of the springtime
    More will come to me then, many things, many hopes,
Dearest the things I have heard of the Father whom I
    Fell silent about, who freshens the wandering times
High in the heights, the Almighty who rules above mountains,
    Soon he will give us heavenly gifts and call forth
Brighter song and the many spirits we need. Oh come soon:
    Hold us, lift us, come now, angels of the year, and you,

## 6

Angels of the house, and into the veins, into all of life's veins
    Enter and Heaven break over all and make nobler,
Younger and nothing that is human and good and not any
    Hour of the day be without cheerful angels and also
Joy such as this when loved ones are found again,
    Such as is fitting for them, hallowed as it ought to be.
Blessing our bread, whom shall I name and when we
    Rest from the life of the day, how shall I offer thanks?
By naming the Highest? A god will not like our mistakes.
    To grasp him our joy is almost too small.
Often we are bound to be silent, we lack holy names,
    Hearts beat and yet speech lags behind.
But music may lend any hour its tones and pleases
    Gods perhaps, should they be drawing near.
Let us have music then, and with that the worry
    Is almost soothed that had entered among our joys.
Worries of this kind, willingly or not, in their souls
    Poets must bear, and often, but others they need not.

# The Rhine
*to Isaak von Sinclair*


   I sat in the dark ivy, at the forest's
Gate, just as the golden noon,
To visit the spring,
Came down the stairs of the Alps
Which are to me the stronghold
The gods built for themselves
After an old opinion, but from where
In secret many a resolution
Reaches men; from there
I learned without expecting it
Of a destiny when my soul
Conversing on this and that
In the warm shade
Had wandered towards Italy
And far away towards the coasts of Morea.

   But now in the mountains
Under the silver summits at a depth
Under cheerful greenery
Where the woods with a shudder
And the peering heads of the peaks
Look down at him, all day, it was there
In the coldest pit
I heard him yammering to be released,
The youth, he was heard as he raged
And railed against Earth his mother
And against the Thunderer who fathered him
By mother and father with pity but
Humanity fled from the place
For it was terrible how he
Lightless in chains
Writhed and raved, that hero.

   It was the voice of the noblest of rivers
The freeborn Rhine
And high at the outset he had other hopes
When he parted from his brothers Ticino and Rhône
And wanted to wander and his royal soul

Drove him impatiently to head for Asia.
But it makes no sense
To wish one's own wishes in the face of fate
But the blindest in this
Are the sons of gods. For men know
Their homes and to beasts it is given
To know where to build, but they
Start out
With souls that want direction.

   Pure origins are a riddle. Even
The poem may hardly disclose them. For what
You began as you will remain
However necessity
And discipline work, and most
Is done by birth
And the ray of light
That greets us newborn.
But where else is there one
More made by a happy nativity
For lifelong freedom and only
To gratify the heart
Than the Rhine
Who was born of the blessed heights
And the holy womb of our earth?

   His voice therefore is exultant.
He never loved mewling
Like other infants in swaddling bands.
When the crooked banks
First crept alongside
And thirstily twining around him
To lead him their way before he knew it
And guard him perhaps
In their own jaws, he laughed
And ripped these snakes asunder
And ran with the spoils and if swiftly
He were not mastered
And made to grow, he must like lightning
Have split the earth, and the woods flee after him
As though enchanted and the hills subsiding.

But a god likes to save his sons
Their fugitive lives, and smiles
When headlong but baulked
By the Alps his rivers bridle
As this one does in the depths.
For purity comes
Out of such a smithy
And it is beautiful then
Leaving the mountains
How he contents himself
Dawdling through Germany and quietening his longing
With works and he ploughs the land
Our father Rhine and nourishes children
In towns he founded.

But he never forgets.
For house and home
And law will perish and the days
Of man become monstrous before
One like the Rhine forgets his beginnings
And the pure voice of his youth.
Who were the first
To spoil the ties of love
And make them fetters?
So overweening that they mocked
Their own justice and surely
The fire of Heaven too and then
Despising human paths
Elected overboldness
And strove to equal the gods.

But the gods have enough
In their own immortality and need
If anything
Heroes and men
And other mortal creatures. For since
The supremely blessed feel nothing themselves
Doubtless another must
If it is permissible to say such a thing
Feel in their name, in sympathy and that
Someone they need; but their judgement is
That he shall topple his house

And mix his dearest and his enemies in one scolding
And bury the old and the new generations under the rubble
Whoever seeks to be like them
And will not suffer the difference, the fool.

   Better for a man to have found
A measured fate
On a safe shore where the memory
Of wanderings still
And suffering sweetly surfaces
To look here and there without rancour
And see the limits
Set him at birth
By God to live within.
He has peace, he is blessed, he is undemanding
For everything he desired,
Heaven's good, of itself
Comes over him smiling, unforced,
Now that he rests from his boldness.

   I am thinking of demigods.
And should I not know them for whom
My heart has often quickened with love and longing?
But one whose soul like yours, Rousseau,
Endured and became invincible
To whom sure sense was given
The gift of hearing and speech
To speak like the god of wine
From such abundance
Holy, foolish and according to no law
Which is the language of the purest in heart
And the good understand it but it smites
The heedless, the sacrilegious hirelings
Rightly with blindness, what
Shall I call such a stranger?

   The sons of the earth are, like the mother,
All-loving, for which they receive
Everything effortlessly and are blessed.
It startles a man
With fear
When he thinks of the heaven

His loving arms have piled
On his shoulders
And the burden of joy.
Then often what seems to him best
Is Biel, the lake, the breezy greenery,
In woodland shade
Where the light does not burn
And poor in tunes and cares
To learn like a beginner from the nightingales.

And to rise from the sacrament of sleep
How good that is, waking
From the cool of the woods, at evening then
To approach the milder light
When he who built the mountains
And drew the rivers their paths
Has filled the sails of our busy lives
So poor in breath
And steered us, smiling, with his breezes
When he too rests and towards
His pupil now the maker
Finding more good than bad
Towards this present earth
The day inclines. –

Then men and gods will have their bridal feast
Everything that lives will celebrate
And fate for a while
Is entirely even-handed.
And the fugitives look for shelter
And the brave a sweet sleep
But the lovers are
What they were, they are
At home where flowers delight in
Harmless fire and the foreboding trees
Are breathed about by the spirit, but people at odds
Have turned in their tracks and are hurrying
To take hands now before
The friendly light
Goes down and the night comes.

And some this hurries by
But others
Retain it longer.
The eternal gods
Are full of life for ever; but unto death
A man also
Can retain the best in mind
And crown his life with it.
To everyone his measure.
Unhappiness is hard
To bear, but happiness harder.
One wise man managed
From midday to midnight
And until the morning shone
To keep his wits at the banquet.

Sinclair, on a burning path among pines
Or in the darkness of an oakwood clad
In steel or among the clouds if God
Appears you will know him since you know
In your strength his and his goodness and he never smiles
The smile of power but you discover it
In daylight when
Feverish and chained it seems
The quick of life or else
At night when everything mixes
Without order and the ancient
Chaos returns.

# Patmos

*for the* Landgraf *of Homburg*


The god is near and
Hard to grasp but
Where there is danger some
Salvation grows there too.
Eagles live
In the dark and the sons of the Alps
Cross over the abyss without fear
On lightly built bridges.
Since, then, the summits of time
Are piled around us
And our loved ones are
Close and fainting
On peaks far apart
Oh give us innocent water
Give us wings that we
Loyally go over and return.

Those were my words, and quicker
Than I had supposed and far
To where I had never thought I should come
A spirit took me away
From home. The shadowy wood
And the longing streams
Of home were darkening
In twilight when I left
And I never knew the lands;
But soon in a light
That was fresh, and mysteriously
In a golden smoke
Grown rapidly
With the strides of the sun
And the scent of a thousand summits

Asia flowered, and blinded I looked
For something I knew
Unused as I was to the broad streets where
Down from Tmolus
Pactolus comes in gold

And Taurus stands and Messogis
And the garden full of flowers,
A quiet fire; but high in the light
The silver snow blossoms
And showing the life eternal
On unclimbable walls
The ancient ivy grows and the majestic
God-built palaces are borne
By living columns
Of cedar and laurel.

But around the doors of Asia
Here and there
Over the uncertain levels of the sea
Shadowless roads in any number go,
But the boatman knows the islands.
And when I heard
That one lying near
Was Patmos
It made me long
To put in there
And approach the dark cave there.
For Patmos is splendid
Not as Cyprus is
That abounds in streams
Nor like any other but

In a poorer house
Is nevertheless
Hospitable and when
Shipwrecked or
Crying for home or
The departed friend
Some stranger
Nears her she welcomes the sound and her children
The hot grove's voices
And where the sand falls and the surface of the field
Cracks, those noises too
Hear him and give a loving echo
Of the man's laments. So once
She cared for God's
Beloved seer who was blessed in his youth

With the company of
The son of the Highest, they went
Inseparably for the Thunderbearer loved
The disciple's simplicity and *he* was attentive
And saw the countenance of God exactly
When at the mystery of the vine
They sat together at supper and the Lord
Foreknowing and at peace from his large soul
Spoke out his death and the last love
For at that time
There was no end of his words of loving-kindness
And good cheer when he saw the world
Angry. For everything is good. Thereupon he died. Much might
Be said about this. And one last time his friends
Saw him in the look of victory, at his most joyful

But mourned since now
It was evening, and they were astounded
And a decision was weighing in their hearts
But they loved life in the sun
And were loath to leave the sight of the Lord
And home. But it
Was driven into them like fire in iron
And the shadow of their beloved kept them company.
Therefore he sent them
The spirit and the house
Shook and God's turbulence rolled
Thundering into the distance over
Their guessing heads when,
Thinking heavily, they were assembled
Like sentenced heroes

And he appeared
Once more to them and departed.
For the sun put out his light now,
The royal day, and snapped
The straight beams of his sceptre himself
With a god's pain
And intended returning
When the time is right. It would have been wrong
Later, abrupt and untrue,
The work of mankind, and it was a joy

From now on
To live in the loving night and preserve
In simple eyes, unflinching,
Abysses of wisdom. And lively images
Are verdant under the mountains too.

   But the way God scatters life
Hither and thither to the uttermost
Is terrible. Not only to lose
Sight of the dear friends' faces
And far over the mountains go
Alone when between two
The heavenly spirit was recognised
In unison and not as a thing to come but
Present and tugging at the hair
When suddenly
Hurrying away the god looked back at them
And swearing an oath
To hold him as though bound
Henceforth by golden cords
They said the worst and took one another's hands –

   But when besides he dies
On whom more than on anyone
Beauty hung so that his shape
Worked a miracle and the gods
Pointed him out and when they are left
For ever a riddle to one another
And cannot comprehend and yet they lived
Together in the memory and when it takes away
Not only the sand or the willow trees
And seizes the temples but down the wind
Goes the honour of the demigod and his kin
And the Highest himself
Thereupon averts his countenance
And nowhere in the sky is anything
Immortal to be seen nor on
The verdant earth – tell me, what is this?

   It is the throw of the winnower when he catches
Corn in the fan
And flings it towards daylight over the floor.

The chaff falls at his feet but
The wheat gets through
Nor is that bad if some
Is lost and the living sound
Of speech disperses for
God's work resembles ours and he does not wish
Everything at once.
True, there is iron in the shaft
And glowing resin in Etna
So I would have the riches
To shape a shape and see
Him how he was, the Christ,

    And what if one spurred himself and waylaid me
Conversing sadly when I was defenceless
So that I marvelled and such a servant
Wanted to copy the image of the god –
In his anger once I saw the Lord
Of Heaven visible. Not to be anything myself. Only
To learn. They are kind, but what they loathe above all,
So long as they rule, is falseness and nothing
Human counts then among mankind.
For who has governance? The fated
Gods and their work
Proceeds of itself and is hurrying to an end.
For when the triumph of Heaven rises higher
The strong will name him like the daystar
They will name God's joyful son

    As a watchword, and here is the staff
Of song beckoning him down.
Now nothing is ordinary. The dead
Not coarsened yet
Will be woken. But many eyes
That are shy of looking are waiting to see
The light. They will not flower
When the beams are sharp
Although a golden bridle holds in their eagerness.
But when as though
Through shielding brows
Away from the world
A gently luminous power falls from the scriptures

Glad of the grace they may try themselves
On those quiet glances.

    If now the gods, as I
Believe, love me
How much more you
For I know this:
The will
Of the eternal Father weighs
With you. His sign is quiet
In the thundering sky. And one stands beneath it
His whole life long. For Christ still lives.
And all the heroes who are the Father's sons
Have come and holy scriptures
From him and the deeds of the earth
Explain his lightning still,
A race that cannot be halted. But he is there. For known
Unto God are all his works from the beginning.

    The honour of the gods has been
Too long, too long invisible.
For they must almost
Guide our fingers and do
A shameful violence to wrest the hearts from us.
For the gods want, all of them, oblations
And neglect has done us
Nothing but harm.
We have served Mother Earth
And lately the light of the sun
In ignorance, but the Father
Governing all
Loves best that we tend
The solid letter and make good sense
Of what we have. And German poets try to.

# Remembrance

The nor'easter is blowing
The dearest of the winds
To me since it fires the sailor's
Spirit and promises a prosperous voyage.
But go now and greet
The lovely Garonne
And the gardens of Bordeaux
At a place where the banks are abrupt
And the path goes along and down
Into the river the stream drops but
Over it looks out a noble pair
Of oaks and white poplars.

I am mindful of it still and how
The elms in a copse incline
Their broad crowns over the mill
But a fig-tree grows in the yard.
On holidays
There the brown women walk
On silken ground
At the March time when
Day and night are equalized
And over the leisurely paths
Heavy with golden dreams
Drowsing breezes pass.

Now let me have
Full of the dark light
A scented glass
So that I rest; for sleep
Would be sweet among shades.
It is not good
To have our souls
Emptied by mortal thinking. But talk
Is good, with one another, and to speak
The heart's opinion and to hear
Abundantly of days of love
And deeds that have happened.

But where are the friends? Bellarmin
With his companion? Some
Are shy of going to the source
For riches begin
In the sea. And they
Like painters bring together
The beauties of the earth and take to
Winged war if they must and live
In loneliness, years at a time, beneath
The leafless mast, their nights
Not lit by the city's holidays
Nor music nor the dances of a native place.

    But now the men
Have gone to the people of India
Past the airy point
And the vineyard hills
Where the Dordogne comes down
And together with the superb
Garonne as wide as the sea
The river leaves. But the sea
Takes memory and gives it
And love, too, busily engages our gaze
But the poets found what lasts.

# The Ister

  Come now, fire,
For we are ravenous
To see the day
And when the proof
Has flung us to our knees
We may hear the forests in uproar.
We have sung our way from the Indus
A long way and
From the Alpheus, we have searched
Years for what would serve.
Lacking wings
No one can reach across
Straight to the next
And come to the other side.
But here we shall build.
For rivers dig up
The land. And when things grow
By them and beasts go down
To them in summer to drink
So people may.

  They call this river the Ister.
His course is beautiful. The columns' foliage
Burns and moves. They stand upright
In the wilds, together; and over them,
A second measure, the roof
Juts from the rocks. Which is why
The Ister invited Heracles
Who shone on Olympus
Far off and came
From the hot Isthmus
Looking for shade. Down there
They were full of fire but for the head
Coolness is needed too, so he came here
To these sources of water
And tawny banks
And the high scents and the blackness
Of fir-forests where in the depths
A hunter strolls

At noon and growth is audible
In the Ister's resinous trees.

But he seems almost
Reversing and
Must come, I think,
From the East
And much
Might be said about that. And why
Does he cling to the hills so? The other,
The Rhine, went off
Sideways. Never for nothing
Do rivers run in the drylands. Then for what? To be a sign,
Nothing else, a forthright sign, and carry the sun
And moon inseparably in mind
And continue by day and by night and keep
The gods warm together.
That is why rivers
Delight the Almighty too. How else
Could he come down? And the earth's green places
They are the children of Heaven. But he,
The Ister, seems too patient,
Unfree, almost derisive. For when

The day should start
In his youth, when he begins
To grow, when the other there
Pushes his pride high and grinds the bit
Like a colt and the air
For miles hears his tumult
This one contents himself;
But rock needs gashes
And the earth furrows
Or how should we plant and dwell?
But what that river is up to
Nobody knows.

# Mnemosyne

Ripe and dipped in fire and cooked
Are the fruits and proved on earth and the law now is
That everything enters, snake-like,
Prophetically, dreaming on
The hills of Heaven. And things
Want keeping like
A burden of faggots on the shoulders
A lot of things. But the paths
Are wicked. The imprisoned
Elements and old
Laws of the earth go wrong
Like horses. And always
There is a longing to dissolve. But a lot
Wants keeping. Faith.
Let us look neither before nor behind, instead
Be cradled as though
On the lake in a rocking boat.

But the things we love? We see
The sunshine on the ground and the dry dust
And the shadows of the woods are homely and the smoke
Flowers from the roofs about the old crowns
Of towers peacefully. The day's marks are good
When something of Heaven
Has hurt our souls with contradictions.
For snow like lilies of the valley
Denoting nobleness
Wherever it be is shining on
The Alps' green meadows
Half and half where a traveller
Speaking of the cross set for the dead
High on the road
Rages forward full
Of the far future
With his companion, but what is this?

At the fig tree my
Achilles died
And Ajax lies

By the sea caves
By the streams that neighbour Scamander.
With a roaring in the temples once, after
The invariable custom of
Unmoved Salamis, great
Ajax died abroad,
Patroclus though in the king's armour. And others died,
Many besides. But on Cithaeron lay
Eleutherae, Mnemosyne's city. She too when God
Put off his coat at evening
She too undid her hair. For he riles the gods
Who will not compose himself
And spare his soul, although he must; and grief
Like him goes wrong.

# Tears

Heaven's love, should I ever forget that love
   And the kindness of heaven, should I...and you
      They visited with fire and are full
         Of ash already and desolate and

Lonely, beloved islands that were the eyes
   Of the fabled places, you solely now
      Concern me, shores where idolatrous
         Love paid the price, but only to Heaven.

For all too gratefully they served, those blessed
   With life there in the days of beauty and
      The heroes in a rage of life, and trees
         In plenty and the cities stood, were there

To be seen like a man in the senses; now
   The heroes are dead and the islands of love
      Almost disfigured. So love must be
         Everywhere, foolish and at a loss.

Oh may the light of my eyes not be put out
   Wholly with tears and death not shame me and let
      A memory live after though I
         Am weak now, robbed and deluded by tears.

# Ganymede

The boy sleeps, the familiar of mountains, why?
   Dull, at odds, freezing on the bare bank.
      Has he forgotten the grace he had
         At Heaven's tables, when they were thirsty?

Down here he seems not to recognise the angels
   Nor the airs playing more sharply among the rocks
      And the word a travelled man sends him,
         The old breathing word, does it never arrive?

Oh, *now* it sounds! It strikes in him like water
   Deep, coming up, as once before high among
      The rocks, sleeping, and now in a rage
         He cleanses himself of the shackles now

Now races, who seemed slow, and sloughs off the dross,
   Takes, breaks and casts them broken aside
      Happy with rage, so easy, on either
         Staring bank, and at this stranger's

Own voice the flocks leap to their feet, the woods
   Move and deep in the land, distant, the river's
      Being is heard and the spirit again
         Shudders to life in the navel of the earth.

The spring. And everything after its fashion
   Flowers. But he is not with us now, he went
      Away, he wandered, for they were all
         Too kind, again he speaks heavenly language.

# Chiron

Light, thoughtful light, where are you, who always must
    Go aside at times, where are you? My heart
        Is awake but the astounding night
            Thwarts me in anger still. I used to go

For herbs into the woods, I was soft and shy,
    I listened by the hill and never in vain,
        Never once did your birds deceive me
            And almost all too eagerly you came

Wanting the refreshment of my garden or
    A foal or my counsel for your heart, oh light
        Where are you? My heart has woken but
            Still I am shut in by the heartless night.

I remember what I was. The earth gave me
    Its first bouquet of saffron, corn and thyme.
        I learned under the cool stars, at least
            Such things as we can put a name to. Then

He came, the upright man, the demi-god, the hind
    Of Zeus, and took the magic from the wild fields
        And saddened them. Now I sit alone
            From one hour to the next and my thoughts

Make figures from clouds of love and the wet earth
    For poison is between us, and I listen
        Into the distance whether perhaps
            A friendly saviour might not come to me.

Then I hear the chariot of the Thunderer
    Often at noon, approaching, I know him best,
        His house reverberates and the ground
            Is cleansed and my pain echoes after him.

I hear my saviour in the night, I hear
    Him killing, my liberator, and I peer
        As though in visions down at the earth
            Luxuriant with growth like a fierce fire;

The days come and go, and when one watches them,
  The good and the bad, and suffers, when one is
    Two in shape and there is nobody
      At all who knows what would be for the best

That is the thorn of the god working, for how
  Could one love otherwise divine injustice?
    Then the god comes home and settles in
      And we are face to face and the earth is changed.

Day! Day! Now the willows can breathe again
  Along my streams, and drink. The eyes have light
    And there are proper footings, and as
      A regent, spurred, local and home, you shine

Out in your self, my errant star of the day,
  And the earth also, a peaceful cradle, shines
    And the house of my fathers who were
      Not citizens and went in clouds of beasts.

Now take a horse and clothe yourself in armour
  And take up the light spear, child. The prophecy
    Will hold and with it will appear my
      Returning Heracles, so waited for.

# Ages of Life

Euphrates' cities and
Palmyra's streets and you
Forests of columns in the level desert
What are you now?
Your crowns, because
You crossed the boundary
Of breath,
Were taken off
In Heaven's smoke and flame;
But I sit under clouds (each one
Of which has peace) among
The ordered oaks, upon
The deer's heath, and strange
And dead the ghosts of the blessed ones
Appear to me.

# Half of Life

The land with yellow pears
And full of wild roses
Hangs into the lake
O gracious swans
And drunk with kisses
You plunge your heads
Into the holy, the sobre water.

Alas, for where in winter
Shall I come by flowers and where
The sunlight and
The shade of the earth?
The walls stand
Speechless and cold, the wind
Clatters the weathervanes.

## 'As birds slowly pass over'

As birds slowly pass over
The prince of them looks ahead
And coolly around
His breast the happenings waft
And he is in silence high
In the air and below him lies
Richly shining the wealth of the lands and with him are
For the first time his young ones looking for conquest.
With strokes of his wings however
He calms.

## 'As upon seacoasts'

As upon seacoasts when the gods
Begin to build and the work of the waves
Ships in unstoppably wave
After wave, in splendour, and the earth
Attires itself and then comes joy
A supreme, tuneful joy, setting the work to rights,
So upon the poem
When the wine-god points and promises
And with the darling of Greece,
Seaborn, veiling her looks,
The waves beach their abundance.

# Home

And nobody knows

Let me walk meanwhile
And pick wild berries
To quench my love of the earth
On her paths

Here where—
                and the thorns of roses
And lime trees scenting sweetly by
The beeches, at noon, when in the dun cornfield
Growth rustles through the straight stalks
And the corn bows sideways at the neck
Like autumn, but now beneath the high
Vault of the oaks where I wonder
And ask upwards the bell
Well-known
Strikes from a distance, golden notes, at the hour
When the birds wake again. Wellbeing.

## 'For when the juice of the vine'

For when the juice of the vine
The mild growth looks for shade
And the grape grows under the cool
Vaulting of the leaves
A strength to the men
Sweetsmelling to the girls
And bees
When they are touched by the spirit of the sun
Drunk on the scent of spring
They chase it
Driven but when
Beams burn they home
With a hum, full of presentiment
                          above
        the oak rustles

## 'On pale leaves'

On pale leaves
The grape rests, the hope of wine, so on the cheek
The shadow rests of a golden earring
Worn by a girl.

And I'm to stay single
But the calf
Easily tangles in the rope
It broke.

Working

But the sower loves to see
One fallen asleep
In daylight
Over her darning.

A German mouth
Lacks euphony
But sweetly
On a prickly beard
A rush of kisses.

## 'When over the vineyard'

When over the vineyard it flames
And black as coal
The vineyard looks around the time
Of autumn because
The pipes of life breathe more fierily
In the shadows of the vine. But
It is beautiful to unfold our souls
And our short lives

# The Eagle

My father travelled, he was on
The Gotthard where
The rivers go down and went
Aslant to Etruria and also
Straightways over the snow
To Olympia and Haemus
And where Athos casts
Its shadow at the caves of Lemnos.
But comes in the first place
From the Indus with my mother
Among the spice forests.
But our first father
He was a sharp-eyed king
Who crossed the sea
Shaking his golden head
At the mystery of the waters
As the clouds steamed red
Above the ship and the beasts
Looked dumbly at one another
And wanted foddering, but
The hills indeed stand still:
Where shall we rest?

We have the rocks
For pasture, the drylands
To drink and for our meat
We have the wet.
Who wants a dwelling-place
Let it be by steps
And where a little house hangs down
Rest by the water
And what you have
Is to draw breath
And sleep restores
What you drew up
By day. For where
The eyes are covered and
The feet are bound
There you will find it.
Where will you see...?

## 'Where we began'

Where we began it was
The abyss, we went
Like the lion vexed and doubtful
For men have sharper senses in
The desert
Fire, they are
Drunk with light and the spirit of beasts
Is with them. But soon my voice
Will go about like a dog in the heat of the day
In the alleys of the gardens where people live
In France
But Frankfurt, to speak of it after man's
The print of nature's
Shape is this
Earth's navel, these times too
Are time and coloured German.
But above the slope of my gardens
There is a wild hill. Cherry trees. But a sharp breath wafts
Around the holes of the rocks. And here I am
And everything with me. But a tree bends
A miraculous slim nut-tree
Over the water-sources and...Berries like coral
Hang on the branches over wooden pipes
From which
Of corn once but, to confess it now, the assured song of
      flowers when
New culture from the town where
To the point of pain in the nostrils
The smell of lemons rises and oil out of Provence and this
Gratitude
Gascony gave me. But, still to be seen, what tamed and
      nourished me was
The pleasure of rapiers and roast meat on the feast days
The table and swarthy grapes and swarthy
                      and glean me, o
You blossoms of Germany, my heart will be
Trustworthy crystal on which
The light is proven when        Germany

## 'Severed and at a distance now'

Severed and at a distance now and in
  The past if I were able still to show you
    Something good and you with a sorrow
      Equalling mine should you still know my face

Then say how might she expect to find you now,
  Your friend: in the gardens where we met again
    After the terror and the dark or
      Here by the rivers of the unspoilt world?

I will say this: there was some good in your eyes
  When in the distances you looked about you
    Cheerfully for once who were a man
      Always closed in his looks and with a dark

Aspect. The hours flowed away. How quiet
  I was at heart thinking of the truth which is
    How separate I would have been, but
      Yes I was yours then and I told you so

Without a doubt and now you will bring and write
  All the familiar things back into mind
    With letters and it happens to me
      The same and I will say all of the past.

Was it spring or summer? The nightingale's
  Sweet singing lived with the other birds that were
    Not far away among the bushes
      And trees were surrounding us with their scents.

On clear pathways, walking among low shrubs
  On sand, we thought more beautiful than anywhere
    And more delightful the hyacinths,
      The tulips, violets and carnations.

Ivy on the walls, and a lovely green
  Darkness under the high walks. In the mornings
    And the evenings we were there and
      Talked, and looked at one another, smiling.

In my arms the boy revived who had been still
   Deserted then and came out of the fields
      And showed me them, with sadness, but the
         Names of those rare places he never lost

And everything beautiful that flowers there
   On blessed seaboards in the homeland that I
      Love equally, or hidden away
         And only to be seen from high above

And where the sea itself can be looked upon
   But nobody will. Let be. And think of her
      Who has some happiness still because
         Once we were standing in the light of days

Beginning with loving declarations or
   Our taking hands, to hold us. Such pity now.
      That was our beautiful daytime but
         Sorrowful twilight followed after it.

You were so alone in the beautiful world,
   Beloved, how often you told me! But you
      Cannot know you were...

# From Sophocles' *Ajax*

*Lines 394-427:*

AJAX.
    Oh night, my light, o Erebus shining at me
    Take me, take
    Me native here, take me. For
    Not to the race of gods nor among
    Everyday men am I
    Fit to look for a help. But I am thrashed
    To death by Zeus'
    Terrible goddess.
    Where must one flee to,
    That being so, where shall I go
    And stay?
    When it withers this side, dear ones,
    And I lie wholly othered
    And wildly out of my mind.
    But let all the army from both sides
    Kill me with their hands.

TECMESSA.
    Unhappy woman. That such a man of sense
    Lets go. He never did before.

AJAX.
    O streams that enter the sea, o caves by the sea, and you
    My little wood hanging over the shore
    A long long time
    You held me up, at Troy,
    Now no more, no more
    Drawing breath. Let a man
    Come to his senses here and remember.
    Alas, by the Scamander, streams
    Kind to the Argives
    One of us you will never
    See again, I speak
    Big words: like him
    Troy saw no other in the host
    That came from Greece
    And my state now
    Is all dishonourable.

CHORUS.

Famous Salamis, somewhere
You dwell among the sea-waves, fortunate,
And anyone may find you.
But I have suffered
A long time now
A same and countless time
On Ida on the grassy pastures
Time has been eating me and I entertain
Bad hopes that soon
I'll chase my elusive death
To earth in Hell.
I have a new enemy, his name:
Ajax, who serves me roughly, oh me, oh my, his
House is a godly madness.
You sent him forth once
Splendidly in a wild
War mood. But now
His brains are all alone and to his dear friends
He is a large sorrow
And the works once of our hands
The high works of our virtue, these have fallen
From favour now with the ill-favoured
Useless sons of Atreus.

True, the mother whom the ageing days
Look after but
Snow-white in years when she hears of his sickness
Something of his madness
She will lament, lament, and not
With the dirge of the grieving nightingale
She won't but shrilly
She'll wail and blows dealt by
Her hands will fall on her breasts
And her head of hair will tumble.

Better to sleep in Hell than be
Sick and good-for-nothing when one of our race
Of tribulated Greeks comes home
No longer master of
His native rage, but beside himself.

O father suffering to an end
What unbearable harm awaits you when
You learn of your child
For time has never brought the like
To light among the Aeacides
This excepted.


*Lines 693-718*

CHORUS.
      I shake with love, good all around, I open.
      O Pan, Pan!
      O Pan! o Pan! be seized by waves from upon
      Cyllene on the rockfirm hill
      In driving snow, appear, o you
      King of the given gods, you gatherer
      And fit together the Nysian steps you
      Taught yourself, and the Cnosian, for me, with me
      Now that I long to dance.
      And you who open over the Sea of Icarus
      King Apollo
      Famous on Delos
      Favour me evermore.
      For Ares has loosed the torment from his eyes.
      Joy, oh joy. And now
      Now Zeus appear in the white light
      Of lovely day driving
      The rapid ships, now that Ajax
      Forgetting his pains
      Ushers to the gods the lovely smoke of sacrifice
      Lawfully serving
      And eminent again.
      For mighty time drags everything away, to make
      It pass. And there is nothing now
      I call unsingable since
      Beyond our hope
      Ajax in his mind
      Has ended his quarrel with the sons of Atreus.

# From Sophocles' *Antigone*

*II.i, lines 349-70*

CHORUS.
  Monstrous, a lot. But nothing
  More monstrous than man.
  For he, across the night
  Of the sea, when into the winter the
  Southerlies blow, he puts out
  In winged and whirring houses.
  And the noble earth of the gods in heaven,
  The unspoilable tireless earth,
  He rubs it out; with the striving plough
  From year to year
  He does his trade, with the race of horses,
  And the world of the gaily dreaming birds
  He ensnares, and hunts them;
  And the train of wild beasts
  And the Pontos' nature that thrives in salt
  With spun nets
  This knowing man.
  And catches game with his arts
  That sleeps and roams on the mountains.
  And over the rough-maned horse he flings
  The yoke on its neck, and over the mountain –
  Wandering and untamed bull.

*III.ii, lines 835-44 & 852-61*

ANTIGONE.
  See, citizens of my mother country,
  Me going the final way
  And seeing the sun's
  Last light.
  That never again? The god
  Of death who hushes everything
  Is leading me living
  To the banks of Acheron, I am not called
  To Hymen, no wedding song,
  No song of praise sings me but I
  Am married to Acheron.

I have heard she was laid to waste
That Phrygian so full of life
Whom Tantalus dangled, on Sipylus' peaks
She is crouched and shrunk
To a slow stone, they put her in chains
Of ivy and winter is with her
Always, people say, and washes her throat
With snow-bright tears
From under her lids. Like her
Exactly a ghost brings me to bed.


*IV.i, lines 981-1024:*

CHORUS.
Danaë too she had to have
On her body instead of the light of the sky
An iron grid, and bear it.
She lay in the dark
With Death, in chains.
O child, though her birth was high
She counted the strokes of the hours,
The golden strokes, for the Father of Time.

But Fate is terrible, it falls
Like rain on the fighting men and on
The tower and catches
Even the black and ocean-splitting ships
And Dryas' son, the Edonian king,
Whose mouth ran over with insults him
The furious Dionysus apprehended
And buried under mounds of stones.

He wept out almost all his madness so
And his luxuriant rage and groping in madness
With insults on his tongue
He got to know the god
For he vexed the women full of the god
And the flute-playing Muses
And fed the exultant fires.

By skyblue rocks
Where at both ends sea is
There are the Bosphorus shores
And the lap of Salmydessus

Belonging to Thracians; and there
Close to the city the butcher god
Spectated whilst the wild wife
Struck the two sons of Phineus a blinding wound
And it grew dark in the bold orbs of their eyes
With spear pricks, under bloody hands
And needle points.
And thinning to nothing, poor things, they wept
Their poor pain to their mother; they had
An unmarried beginning, but hers
Was the seed of Erectheus
Begun long ago.
In wandering caves
She was reared, in her father's storms, child
Of the North Wind, palled with horses, on the sheer hill,
A daughter of the gods, But on her too
A massive fate rested, child.

## 'In a lovely blue'

In a lovely blue the church spire with its metal cladding flowers. Around it go the screams of the swallows, around it lies the most touching blue. High over it climbs the sun and colours the metal, but above, in the winds, the weather cock crows quietly. If anyone goes down then under the bells, down those steps, life has stillness then, because, when shapes are so separate, the plasticity of man emerges. The windows, through which the bells are sounding, are like gates in their beauty. For since gates are after nature still they have the appearance of trees of the forest. But purity is beauty too. Inside, from a variety, an earnest spirit arises. But so simple are the images, so very holy, that truly one is often fearful of describing them. But the heavenly gods, who are always kind, all together, they own like kingdoms these: virtue and joy. A man may imitate that. May a man, when life is all toil, look up and say: I too will be like that? He may. So long as friendliness, pure friendliness, still lasts in the heart a man may measure himself not unhappily with divinity. Is God unknown? Is he as apparent as the sky? The latter, I should say. It is man's measure. Full of merit, but poetically, man lives on this earth. But the shadow of the night with the stars, if I could say it thus, is not purer than man, who is called an image of God.

*

Is there a measure on earth? There is none. For the Creator's worlds never slow down the course of the thunder. Even a flower is beautiful, since it flowers under the sun. Often in life the eye finds living things that might be called more beautiful than the flowers. Oh, I have known that very well. For to bleed at heart and in one's shape and wholly cease to be, is that pleasing to God? But the soul, as I believe, must remain pure, or the eagle with songs of praise and the voices of so many birds will reach to the sources of power, on wings. It is the being of things, it is their shape. Beautiful brook, how touching you seem, rolling so clearly, like the eye of God, through the Milky Way. I know you well enough, but tears start from the eye. I see a cheerful life flowering around me in the shapes of creation, because, with some justice, I compare it to the lonely pigeons in the churchyard. But people's laughter seems to grieve me, for I have a heart. Should I like to be a comet? Perhaps I would. For they have the speed of birds; their fire is such that they flower and for purity they are like children. Human nature could not presume to wish for anything greater. And the good humour of virtue deserves to be praised by the earnest spirit that blows between the three pillars in the garden. A beautiful girl must crown her head with flowers of myrtle because in her nature and in her feelings she has simplicity. But there are myrtles in Greece.

\*

When a man looks in the mirror and sees his image there, as if in a portrait; it looks like the man. The image of the man has eyes; the moon, on the other hand, light. King Oedipus has an eye too many perhaps. These sufferings of this man, they seem indescribable, unsayable, inexpressible. If that is what the play depicts, that is the reason. But what do I feel if I think of you now? I am pulled as streams are by the ending of something – something that spreads like Asia. Suffering of that sort Oedipus had, of course. Naturally that is the reason. Did Hercules suffer too? Indeed he did. And the Dioscuri in their friendship, did they not bear some suffering too? For to quarrel with God, as Hercules did, that is suffering. And in the envy of this life to share one's immortality, that is suffering too. But to be covered in freckles, to be covered all over with them, that is a sort of suffering too. The beautiful sun is to blame for that: it brings everything out. The sun encourages the young men along their way with its beams as with roses. The sufferings Oedipus bore seem as if a poor man were crying that something was wrong. Son of Laius, poor stranger in Greece! Life is death, and death too is a life.

# Notes

13. **'When I was a boy'**: Written towards the end of Hölderlin's time in Frankfurt, 1797-98; first published 1826. To earn a living, Hölderlin was four times the tutor of young children.

14. **To Diotima**: Unfinished. Probably written 1797 as one of the first of the poems to Susette Gontard; not published until 1908. The phrase 'a loving quarrel' is a key to much of Hölderlin's poetic philosophy.

15. **Diotima**: The expansion, summer 1800, of two strophes written in 1798; first published 1826. Diotima belongs among the Greeks. The poem celebrates them, laments their passing and looks forward to a time in which Diotima would be at home again.

16. **Plea for Forgiveness**: Written 1798, published 1799. The fact is a woman cannot, unlike the moon, resume her old tranquillity.

17. **'Another day'**: Unfinished. Written perhaps as late as spring 1800; first published 1846. An elegy 'Mcnons Klagen um Diotima' ('Menon's lament for Diotima') is a large expansion of this topic.

18. **To the Sun God**: Written 1798, first published 1846. In Hölderlin's mythology we inhabit the night.

19. **To the Fates**: Written 1798, published 1799. This was one of the very few poems Hölderlin's mother showed an interest in: she was worried by it, understandably. In fact he was given more than one summer, but not many more.

20. **Fate. Hyperion's Song**: The poem occurs in the second volume, published 1799, of Hölderlin's novel *Hyperion*. The hero sings it as the ruin of his life is becoming clear.

21. **Sung under the Alps**: Written early 1801 when Hölderlin was in Hauptwil, Switzerland; first published 1802. The proximity of the Alps moved Hölderlin greatly (see also the elegy 'Homecoming'). He felt he was close to innocence. It was in Hauptwil that he learned of the Peace of Lunéville, a brief cessation of hostilities to which he attached large hopes. In the last lines here his poetic vocation seems clear to him.

22-9. **The Archipelago**: This tremendous poem, probably written in the spring of 1800 (first published 1804), opens with an evocation of spring in the Greek archipelago, and its wish throughout is that this literal regeneration should also become a figurative one and that we, in the present, should recover, in our Hesperian mode, the condition of Periclean Athens. The poem re-enacts the rebuilding of the city after the Persians, who had sacked it, were defeated at the Battle of Salamis. That image at the heart of the poem (p.26, *ll*.22ff) is immensely encouraging; but the poem also repeatedly faces up to our loss, to the barbarism of our times and to the precariousness of the poet's existence in them (p.23, *ll.*25 ff.; p.28, *ll.*3ff.; p.27, *ll.*8 ff.) Nevertheless, its constant drive is towards fulfilment, amply imagined in p.28, *ll.*19-39.

p.22, *l.*5: Ionia: the coast of Asia Minor.

p.23, *l.*12: Cayster: a river of Asia Minor entering the Aegean near Ephesus.

*l.*14: According to Ovid (*Metamorphoses*) the Nile fled when Phaeton crashed and set the world on fire.

*l.*31 (and p.25, *l.*33 and p.26, *l.*39): The Acropolis.

*l.*40: Colchis: on the east coast of the Black Sea, where the Argonauts went after the Golden Fleece.

p.24, *ll.*3-4.: The Straits of Gibraltar. The youth is Themistocles, preparing to meet the Persians. He persuaded the Athenians to trust themselves to the sea, and in so doing encouraged democracy, since it was from the lower classes that the sailors for the new navy came and after Salamis they wanted their say. Some years before writing 'The Archipelago' Hölderlin had explicitly associated the wars of Athens and Persia with those of France and reactionary Europe.

*l.*18: The King: Xerxes. Ecbatana: the ancient capital of Media, the summer residence of the Persian kings.

*ll.*27 ff.: After Thermopylae the Greeks withdrew to their last line of defence on the Isthmus of Corinth, and brought back their fleet to Salamis, leaving Athens and the whole of Attica to be sacked. Themistocles forced the outcome then in the narrows of Salamis (BC.480). Hölderlin's account of the battle may be compared with the Messenger's report in Aeschylus' *The Persians*.

p.25, *l.*36: Probably the Stoa Basileios or Royal Portico.

p.26, *l.*14: The Ilissus: a river of Athens, on the south side of the city.

*l.*21: Colonus: where Oedipus came when he was banished from Thebes, its horses and natural beauties are celebrated by Sophocles.

*l.*27: Pentelicus: a mountain to the north-east of Athens famous for its marble quarries.

*l.*34: The Prytaneum: the magistrates' hall.

*l.*37: The Olympeion: the Temple of Olympian Zeus.

p.27, *l.*2: On the headland: at Sunium.

*l.*14: Castalia: a spring under Parnassus, sacred to the Muses.

*l.*18: Tempe: a beautiful valley in Thessaly between Mounts Olympus and Ossa.

*ll.*29-33: These lines name three places famous for prophecy. They are: Dodona, where Zeus spoke through the wind in the oak tree; Delphi, where Apollo spoke through his priestess; and 'the prescient town' of Thebes, home of Tiresias.

p.29, *ll.*3-8: Three important battles. They are: Marathon, BC.490, when the Athenians defeated the Persians; Chaeronea, BC.338, when the Thebans and Athenians were defeated by Philip of Macedon; Thermopylae (under Mount Oeta), BC.480, where the Spartans held out against but were finally slaughtered by the Persians.

**30-32. Homecoming:** Written soon after Hölderlin's return from Hauptwil in April 1801; almost certainly his last elegy; published 1802. The poem is structured by the literal homecoming: the crossing of Lake Constance to Lindau, the journey from there to Nürtingen, the reunion with family and friends. The mood is one of joy and hope, but an undertow of personal sadness is also discernible.

p.31, *l*.26: The Rhine comes out of the mountains and flows through Lake Constance from east to west.

p.32, *l*.8: The Peace of Lunéville, 9 February 1801.

**33-8. The Rhine:** Written 1801, first published 1808. This long poem, in the manner of the Greek poet Pindar, begins as a meditation on the course and nature of the Rhine and continues, after p.35, *l*.20, among the possibilities engendered by that meditation. It turns to Rousseau, a force like the river in Hölderlin's view. Generally, the poem may be said to be about the management of energy, its struggle with form, a 'loving strife'. In the dedication and in the final strophe Hölderlin addresses his close friend Sinclair, a combative and politically active man.

p.33, *l*.15: Morea: The Peloponnese.

*l*.35: Ticino and Rhône: both rise, like the Rhine, in the Gotthard massif. The Ticino flows into Italy, the Rhône into France.

p.34, *l*.1: To head for Asia: the Rhine flows east at first, as far as Chur, then bears conclusively north.

p.37, *l*.5: Biel: Rousseau withdrew there, to an island in the lake, for two happy months in 1765.

p.38, *l*.12: One wise man: Socrates. In the *Symposium* he stays awake all night and his conversation never flags.

**39-44. Patmos:** The poem was finished early in 1803 and first published in 1808. It is addressed to the pious ruler of the little state, near Frankfurt, in which Hölderlin lived after the death of Susette Gontard and until his removal to the clinic in Tübingen. Like 'The Rhine' it derives a wider meditation out of its particular subject. 'Patmos' treats Christ's Ministry and Passion rather as Pindar treats the myths of his age, and struggles to hope for the best in times of absence and benightedness.

p.39, *ll*.1-15: Much of the poem is teased out of the imagery of these opening lines.

p.39, *l*.31 – p.40, *l*.10: A compressed landscape of fabulous Asia Minor: Tmolus, Taurus and Messogis are mountains, Pactolus a river famed in antiquity for its gold.

p.40, *ll*.11-21: The poet-traveller turns his back on the brilliant Ancient World and makes for Patmos, an island of *our* time. Patmos is one of the Dodecanese, in sight of Asia Minor. St John wrote the Apocalypse there. Hölderlin believed him to be the same John who was Christ's disciple and who wrote the Gospel. Between that gospel and Hölderlin's poem there are many points of contact.

**45-6. Remembrance:** Written 1803, first published 1808, the poem is full of remembrance of Bordeaux. The wind, blowing that way, makes the connection.

p.46, *l*.1: Bellarmin: in the novel *Hyperion* he is the recipient of the hero's letters. Hölderlin may have his own friend Sinclair in mind.

*l*.14: India is the source (cf *l*. 3). The early mariners thought to reach it by sailing west.

*l*.15: The airy point: doubtless the Bec d'Ambès, where the Garonne and the Dordogne come together.

**47-8. The Ister:** Written 1803, first published 1916. The Danube was called Ister in classical times. Hölderlin was attracted to the river as a poetic subject because, rising in the Black Forest and emptying into the Black Sea, it connects the modern world with the ancient. Here he dwells particularly on its sluggishness, and compares it with the headlong course of the young Rhine. The poem rises against torpor, conjures up animation.

p.47, *l*.7: Indus: the Sind, a great river of India.

*l*.9: Alpheus: a river of Greece, it flows past Olympia.

*l*.27: Heracles: According to Pindar he fetched the olive from the banks of the Ister and made a sprig of it the prize at the Olympic Games.

p.48, *l*.9: The other: the Rhine.

**49-50. Mnemosyne:** Probably written in the autumn of 1803, first published (but imperfectly) in 1916. Mnemosyne was the mother of the Muses; her name means memory. The poem, like much late Hölderlin, combats the loss of memory and seeks to hold on.

p.49, *l*.36: Achilles: a Greek hero, he died young at Troy.

*l*.37: Ajax: a Greek hero, he also fought bravely at Troy. In a bout of madness he disgraced himself and committed suicide afterwards.

p.50, *l*.2: Scamander: one of the rivers of Troy.

*l*.5: Salamis: Ajax's birthplace.

*l*.7: Patroclus: whilst Achilles sulked Patroclus fought and died wearing his armour.

*ll*.8-9: Eleutherai, Mnemosyne's city, is on the southern slopes of Mount Cithaeron in Boeotia.

**51. Tears:** Written, or revised for publication at least, in December 1803. This poem and the following four, together with another four, were published in 1805 as a group entitled 'Night Songs'. They met with derision. 'Tears' is full of longing for the islands of Greece. The grief it expresses is nearly overwhelming.

**52. Ganymede:** A rewriting into radical and difficult language of an earlier poem entitled 'The shackled River'. Ganymede, a herdsboy on Mount Ida, was taken up to be the gods' cupbearer. In this poem, after a separation, he returns to them as spring comes.

**53-4. Chiron:** Also a rewriting in 1803 of an earlier poem, one entitled 'The blind Bard'. Chiron the Centaur longs for release from suffering. Heracles, who accidentally wounded him with a poisoned arrow, returns now with the news that, despite being the son of a god, he is to be allowed to die.

55. **Ages of Life**: Written or prepared for publication in December 1803. Palmyra, a city in the Syrian desert, was destroyed by the Romans in AD.273. Its ruins were rediscovered by western travellers in 1750. There is an eerie sense of time, destruction and loneliness in this poem.

56. **Half of Life**: Written or prepared for publication in December 1803. The poem is beautifully balanced – before life tilts into winter. When Hölderlin was transported to the clinic in Tübingen he was half way through his life.

57. **'As birds slowly pass over'**: Probably written before 1806, not published until 1916. It is an extended simile wanting the thing it refers to and may be part of a poem never written or lost.

58. **'As upon seacoasts'**: Dates as the last. A complete simile (its two sides running together) and perhaps a complete poem.

59. **Home**: Dates as the last. Unfinished. Here and in the next three poems the sensuousness is remarkable.

60. **'For when the juice of the vine'**: Dates as the last. Unfinished.

61. **'On pale leaves'**: Dates as the last. Unfinished.

62. **'When over the vineyard'**: Perhaps earlier than the last. Not published until 1951. Doubtless belonging in a larger context.

63. **The Eagle**: Written before 1806, first published 1916. This is a poem in the manner of the hymns 'The Ister' and 'Remembrance'. Its geography, from India to the Alps, is one to which all the great hymns contribute. Etruria is Tuscany, Haemus is a mountain in Thrace. The shadow of Mount Athos is said to reach the island of Lemnos, eighty-seven miles to the east, when the sun sets at the solstice. 'The Eagle' is a difficult poem, and unfinished.

64. **'Where we began'**: Probably written before 1806, not published entirely until 1951. The poem, unfinished and very difficult to make whole sense of, is remarkable for the brilliance and sharpness of its memories, particularly those of France; and for its calling Frankfurt, where Susette Gontard lived, the navel of the earth (that being Pindar's term for Delphi).

65-6. **'Severed and at a distance now'**: Probably written after 1806, first published 1921. The poem, unfinished, is associated with very late extensions of the novel *Hyperion* and may be thought of as being spoken by Diotima, though, of course, both she, the heroine of the novel, and her counterpart in real life, Susette Gontard, had died.

**Hölderlin's translations of Sophocles:** Hölderlin translated all his writing life. He was intensely occupied with Sophocles during the winter of 1803-4. His versions of *Oedipus Rex* and *Antigone* (he worked at but never finished *Oedipus at Colonus* and *Ajax*) came out in the spring of 1804 and were taken, by the learned, as conclusive proof of his insanity. He translated in a radical and idiosyncratic way. What I have done here is translate his translations, preserving as much as possible of their beautiful strangeness.

**67-9. Three extracts from *Ajax*:**
1. Ajax went mad with rage when the arms of dead Achilles were awarded as prize to Odysseus and not to him. In his madness, and in the dark, he fell upon a flock of sheep and cattle, thinking they were the Greeks who had slighted him. In this first extract, watched by his wife Tecmessa, he has come to his senses. He grieves over his disgrace.
2. Ajax was from Salamis. Here a chorus of the men who came with him to Troy lament the harm he has done.
3. The Chorus, deceived by a new reasonableness in Ajax's manner, jump to the conclusion that all will be well. In fact, he has decided to kill himself.

**70-72. Three extracts from *Antigone*:**
1. The Chorus celebrates man's extraordinary powers.
2. Antigone has been condemned to death for disobeying Creon. In these two speeches she laments her fate. In the second she compares it to that of Niobe.
3. As Antigone is led away the Chorus recalls some horrific precedents for what she will suffer.

**73-4. 'In a lovely blue':** In Tübingen, 1822-4, Hölderlin was much visited by a young man called Wilhelm Waiblinger. Waiblinger wrote a novel, *Phaëthon*, published 1823, in which, to depict his hero, a mad poet, he used Hölderlin's life and writings as material. This poem, which perhaps should be set out like one of the great hymns, is given as an example of the poet's work and it is almost certainly Hölderlin's, though doubtless contaminated by Waiblinger.